DISHING SOUL FOOD IN THE KITCHEN

Designed for Life

T. T. Carole

ABFL Books

Saint Louis, Missouri

T. T. Carole/ABFL Books
Saint Louis, Missouri

Book Layout © 2017 BookDesignTemplates.com

DISHING SOUL FOOD IN THE KITCHEN – Designed for Life /
T. T. CAROLE. – 2nd edition
ISBN 978-1-7322927-7-2

This book is dedicated to my family and friends who keep me encouraged with their contributions and their trust, honesty, and prayers, whenever I secretly lose heart. It is also dedicated to the memory of my God-fearing parents who laid the foundation for the family and always did their personal best to provide.

I am encouraged that even though I do not know how or whom, someone will be blessed through the body of this work.

"We must recreate an attractive and caring attitude in our homes and in our worlds. If our children are to approve of themselves, they must see that we approve of ourselves."

–MAYA ANGELOU

Contents

Chapter 1

"The law of the Lord is perfect, refreshing the soul. The statutes of
the LORD are trustworthy, making wise the simple" (Psalm 19:7)

The Soul of the Home

In Sipping Tea in the Living Room, as I reminisced about growing up in our family home, I stressed how the living room was like the center of our home. It was the place where we gathered for matters of the heart. It was a place where we coalesced as a family. It was where worldviews formed, ideas nurtured, and character displayed. It was the place where we welcomed guests, celebrated life events, engaged in discussions, and found support in the midst of tragedy and uncertainty. It was an especially important part of the house.

Even though the living room served a particularly important purpose, the kitchen—where we went for nourishment—was probably more important in a sense because this is where the meals are prepared. It is where we are refreshed and satisfied. Moreover, it is where we sup with the Master.

Daddy's Up to Something

The kitchen in our family home was small and busy, yet always neat and clean. I remember the walls being decorated with everything from faux brick to some snazzy, bright yellow paint. The kitchen table was often one with extra leaves, added when it was time for dinner.

Momma used to set the table very nicely for the meal. Then, shortly after daddy came home from work, her expectation was that all who lived in the house are to come and sit around the table to eat.

Some of my older siblings might argue this point with me, but from my memory, momma did most of the cooking in the kitchen. Sometimes daddy would step in with a few creations of his own.

Daddy was from the country and he like to hunt and fish. Whenever he cooked, he cooked something reminiscent of the Deep South, such as hog head cheese, rabbit, squirrel, beef brains, and cow tongue.

One of the most interesting dishes that I remember him cooking was mountain oysters. I was probably nine or ten years old at the time, and daddy was stirring up that meal in the kitchen. "What's that daddy?" I asked. He looked with a sheepish grin on his face and at first offered a polite answer: "mountain oysters", he replied. Well, I was young but had been to school long enough to know what oysters looked like, and that was not it.

"Daddy, that is not an oyster; oysters have shells. That thing did not come out of a shell", I demanded. It was not unlike daddy to engage in a little light humor with us from time to time, so, since I was so smart and persistent, he used this as an opportunity to lay one on me. "Okay", he said; "they're hog nuts." Ugh!

I probably could not fully wrap my head around that expression at the time, but my familiarity with that term came from rough-and-tumble play on and around the playground. It seemed that whether by accident or for spite, whenever a boy was hit or kicked in that area of his body, he would cry out that someone kicked them in his 'mountain oysters'. "That's alright daddy; I'll just have a bowl of cereal."

Fanning the Flames

The kitchen in my grown-up home has gone through many changes; everything from color to style. The backsplash has hosted everything from mirror to faux leather paneling, metal-like panels to wallpaper featuring baskets of apples, or dancing chefs. And, like daddy, when I am in there, I enjoy whipping up some interesting meals at times—though none as interesting as his.

Aesthetically, my kitchen looks fine; however, this is one room where I am never satisfied with the decor. This is the room where I have an insatiable desire for change and a craving to do a little more.

I believe that the uneasiness here can be likened to the sometimes restlessness of my soul where it sometimes feels like there is a fire burning deep within[1] while I work out my salvation with fear and trembling[2].

Even though I believe that I am safe, sealed, and secure, l still strive to be all that God intends for me to be. Still striving to let Him do His work in and through me to fulfill his good purpose without my fleshly interference[3].

Yet when I thirst or grow weary, I need to retreat to the inner sanctuary of my soul where I can sup with and be fed by Him. By His spirit, he will open his hand to feed me, and provide nourishment to sustain me. My salvation comes from Him.[4]

> "...his word is in my heart like a fire, a fire shut up in my bones"
>
> ~ JEREMIAH 20:9

Tips and Tricks for Kitchen Design

Simple Crab Fried Rice Recipe

Ingredients

- 3 pouches Uncle Ben's Ready Rice Jasmine (approximately 6 cups)
- 2 eggs (beaten)
- 3 cloves chopped garlic
- 2-3 chopped green onions
- 3-5 tablespoons House of Tsang Stir-Fry Oil (infused with garlic, onion, and herbs for high-heat cooking)
- 1 teaspoon ground white pepper
- 1 cup crab real meat (Bumble Bee brand in refrigerated seafood section)
- 1 English cucumber
- 1 lime
- Parsley or cilantro

Cooking Instructions
(Tip: Because high heat is required for cooking, chop, measure, and separate ingredients into prep bowls in advance)

- Microwave Uncle Ben's Ready Rice according to instructions. Leave in microwave to keep warm until ready to use;
- Heat wok until hot; add oil;
- Add rice and garlic to hot wok (chopped garlic tends to burn quickly it is best to add it with the rice). Stir constantly to brown;
- Move browned rice up the sides of the wok, leaving a hole in the center;
- Stir in eggs to scramble; (add more oil as needed)
- Bring rice back to center of wok and mix with eggs;
- Add crabmeat; stir until thoroughly mixed and warmed;
- Add white pepper to taste;
- Remove mixture from heat; stir in chopped green onions to wilt;
- Garnish a serving dish with thinly sliced English cucumbers and lime wedges; add rice mixture to center;

- Sprinkle with parsley or cilantro; serve immediately.

Chapter 2

"Then the LORD God formed man from the dust of the ground and breathed into his nostrils the breath of life, and man became a living being." ~ Genesis 2:7

The Perfect Layout

Many of us might experience the amazement of either throwing a party or attending a gathering and witnessing the strange dynamic that no matter how limited the space, the guests slowly trickle into the kitchen and linger there with much joy and excitement.

In the natural, the making of that phenomenon, for the host, might present itself as a source of contention or frustration—especially, while preparations are still ongoing, and the workspace vanishes because of the mass of the ensuing crowd. However, amazement turns to wonderment whenever God, the space planner, rests his 'thumb' on a situation.

You Asked for What?

A few years ago, while on a personal spiritual journey, I conducted an experiment, which resulted in my feeling a real sense of aggravation and rebellion.

Single and bemoaning the fact that I was growing older, and possibly less attractive, not only to a potential mate, but to people in general. Thus, I did what people do: I panicked.

So, there was I, every morning, drowning in my self-made despair because of the perception that the beauty of youth was fading, all while trying to be more spiritually mature and aware. To counter the effects of these thoughts on aging, I sought the assist of God, my Higher Power.

Now, having grown even older in years, a little wiser in heart, and more mature in spirit, I can honestly say that looking back on that time, I know now that what I needed was a big dose of reality, a different set of expectations, and a newly worded story to tell myself. Nevertheless, without the wisdom of newfound years, back then, I did what I thought I should do.

We are instructed to ASK (ask, seek, and knock)[5]; admonished to not become anxious about things of which we have little to no control; encouraged to let our requests be made known to God[6]; and moreover, assured that God is a rewarder of us who seek him[7].

During the time of this distress, I was nonetheless confident in what I believe to be the word and promises of God and mustering up the courage to confront this thing head on, I took the matter to His door.

So, there I was enmeshed in the quagmire of my thoughts that led to the perception that the beauty of youth was fading. I was messed up yet encouraged by my belief that He is who He says He is and can do what He says He can do. So, there I prayed every morning: literally, specifically, sincerely, and unashamedly. I prayed in comfort, and with assurance and great expectations.

Though the prayer that I prayed could possibly be misinterpreted or even frowned upon by some as a prayer of vanity and insecurity, nevertheless, I prayed with much delight[8] because my unstated purpose (so says my now-mature self), ultimately, was to be a beautiful witness for the Lord.

When I prayed, I asked God the Father to manifest His Spirit within me; to magnify His glow and become so blindingly beautiful that wherever I went, people would be compelled to look past my aging features and see, not me, but Him instead.

I believe that my prayer proved to be acceptable to God and He did in fact answer. I believe that He moved and manifested the beauty of his Spirit within me just as I had asked, and he gave me a charge and expected me to perform; however, I was caught off guard, and this is where things start to get a little complicated.

A Double Portion

Essentially, by asking God to expose more of Him through me, I was asking him to renovate my soul and expand my territory. Much like the Prophet of old, I asked to be doubly blessed in my life and personal ministry, which turned out to be a hard thing or too much for me at the time.

I proved to be woefully unprepared for the new addition that I sought because rather than welcoming the attention for which I prayed, I, instead rebelled.

My rebellion was not against God because I was too busy being annoyed to connect the dots between my prayer and His power. My rebellion, instead, was against what I interpreted as a constant flow of interruptions by people invading my space during my self-established quiet times.

However, assessing those interruptions from a more mature perspective, I now understand that those instances of being interrupted were the attractions for which I prayed. I now understand that those were chances for me to reflect the beauty of God by using my eyes to look upon someone with kindness without passing judgment about who they are or how they look. Or, by using my ears to listen to someone complain about their situation, then trying to leave them with an encouraging word. Moreover, by using my heart to empathize with a hurting soul (by way of a reassuring look, a kind word, or a warm embrace) whether they were acting out or hiding their deep-seated pain and scars under a well-manicured facade.

In his 1968 "Drum Major Instinct" sermon, Dr. Martin Luther King, Jr. addressed the deep desire that lies under the surface for most of us. He suggests in the sermon that through our overtures and actions, we seek a distinction, or a desire to be important. He said that, that desire was like a "basic impulse" in most humans. He later admonished, in the same sermon that people should not seek to be celebrated by others because of the 'good' things we might do; rather we should humbly celebrate doing the things we might do for others with a view toward the Kingdom for a greater reward.

The Fork in the Road

Up until the time of receiving the "extra" gift and charge, I tended to be a very private and introspective person. Whenever I was out and about—whether shopping or just strolling around the block—I always liked to use those times to process things, without interruption, and think big thoughts about the issues of the day. This all seemed to change with my answered prayer.

What once was a time for quiet meditation while selecting the best cuts of meat for my budget, turned into a game of 'name that meat' while encountering shoppers who might have left their glasses at home and could not read the label, or just did not have a clue about the different types, grades, or cuts of meat.

What was a time to ponder problems and brainstorm solutions while at the mall, trying to pick the shirt, skirt, dress, or pants best suited for my body type, turned into episodes of 'What Not to Wear', as a result of a flow of interruptions by ladies (and sometimes men) desperately trying to put together an outfit for their Women's Day Program, or some other event.

One of my favorites is probably when what would normally be a time for creating fantasies or dreaming big dreams while browsing around in the second-hand store, turned into episodes of 'Flea Market Flip' by good-hearted, bargain hunters wondering if it is possible to turn a small chair into a footstool, or an old console television into a cool aquarium.

Or what once was a time of self-assessment, evaluation, and reflection while in a checkout line anywhere, or on public transportation going to or from work, turned into sessions of dealing with the demons in my own mind as my attention turned to fear while recalling scenes from Denzel Washington's movie, "Fallen". That left me thinking that anybody who touched me might infect me with an unwelcome spirit. Needless-to-say; in my mind, people were standing excessively close or seated too nearby.

Last, but not least, so as not to belabor the point, when sleeping in at home and the phone rings. Reluctantly, picking up to find on the other end a lonely older gentleman who mistakenly dialed my number while desperately trying to reach his indolent son who last he recalled, worked at a nearby business with a similar number.

These events seemed to go on for a while, and in ignorance, I started to grow annoyed. I know that either one or even the sum of them all is not that unusual, but at the time, the intrusions were more than enough.

I can now imagine that God had his "thumb" on the scales of the multiplicity of those situations and was working on preparing this space as I asked. I believe He has since rearranged some things on the inside after laying the groundwork for an upgraded design and greater purpose. And, like most renovations when a space is under construction, there usually is cause for some stress and dismay that comes with the structure being gutted, sealed, and made off limits. However, when the work is closer to completion, everything gets better.

It took a brief season of isolation before I was able to connect the dots between what I asked, what was His will, and how He answered. However, as I continue to grow into the ministry that He has prepared for me, I realize that my soul should not only be bright and beautiful, it also should be welcoming and spacious enough to nourish others with appetizers of presence, love, and understanding that are enjoyed before him.

Thank God that I can now say that the kitchen is open, and all intrusions are welcome.

Tips and Tricks for Kitchen Design

The Basics

If we are thinking about redesign, the kitchen is, by far, the one room in the home where we will realize the best return on investment and will get the most bang for our bucks. Getting this one right, however, requires giving a lot of thought to the needs of the household, the most efficient use of the space, surfaces, appliances, and the family flow.

Aside from cabinetry, the other things to consider are the layout, backsplash, countertops, and flooring. While the layout might be somewhat fixed, updating the other areas can be accomplished relatively inexpensively.

Know Your Kitchen

The layout of most kitchens follows one of these four basic shapes: Galley, L-Shaped, U-Shaped, or Peninsula (G-Shaped).

A Galley kitchen layout is defined by two straight-line countertops, work surfaces and major appliances placed parallel to each other on opposite walls.

An L-Shaped kitchen layout is defined by countertops, appliances, and work surfaces that are aligned along two adjoining walls.

A U-Shaped kitchen layout is defined by countertops, work surfaces and appliances aligned on three adjoining walls: and

A Peninsula (G-Shaped) kitchen layout, like the U-Shaped, is defined by countertops, work surfaces and appliances aligned on three adjoining walls; however, with the addition of an extended counter that separates the kitchen from the dining area.

5 Budget-friendly Ideas for Refreshing Surfaces

Cabinetry. Rather than replacing cabinets, have them refaced and update hardware. If the kitchen is small, consider replacing upper cabinet with open shelving; checkout www.ikea.com for some great ideas.

Backsplash. Change the tone or feel of the kitchen with a creative backsplash. Rather than the expense and mess of tile, consider:

- Peel-and-stick, faux glass, tin, or tiles.
- Waterproof, washable wallpaper.
- Faux brick or stone paneling.
- High gloss paint and stencil in designs such as words or your favorite things.

If there is existing tile on the wall, consider updating them by applying decals of your favorite things.

Countertops. To refresh countertops that are in otherwise good condition consider, painting them to get the high-end look of granite by using paint kits such as the Rust-oleum® Countertop Transformations, or Giani Granite Countertop Paint Kit.

Flooring. Vinyl floor covering come in a beautiful array of styles and patterns and are easy to install over just about any surface.

Chapter 3

I pray that out of his glorious riches he may strengthen you with power through his Spirit in your inner being, so that Christ may dwell in your hearts through faith."

~ Ephesian 3:16, 17a

Power

Before we entered what we now know as this age of higher awareness of the wear and tear that we impose on this planet. And, before we advanced in mindfulness of the way we use, abuse, and waste resources to the detriment of our human ecosystem. Moreover, before we started paying attention to the over-production of greenhouse gases and the way they might affect the stability of the world around us, powering a well-equipped kitchen required lots of energy. Even so, some of the energy produced went to waste due to much inefficiency.

Nowadays, energy efficiency is the basis upon which most manufacturers design and build their products, and powering the kitchen is, therefore, less wasteful, or harmful to our environment.

In time, as technologies continue to advance, power conservation achieved through thoughtful design may well result in an affect that is less of a detriment to that over which we have stewardship and dominion, and more of a way of celebrating the magnificent, beautiful, and plentiful earth, entrusted, delicately, to our care[9].

However, in spite of this ever-changing world and things of this world—whether for the 'good' or 'bad'—as Harry David Thoreau once said, "What lies behind us and what lies ahead of us are tiny matters compared to what lives within us." This brings to mind the delightful proposition floating around in many Christian circles, of the 'God-shaped hole' that is said the Creator purposefully placed inside of every living, human soul.

The God-shaped hole is not just any hole. It is not a hollowed out, one-size-fits-all type of deal either. Rather, it is said to be one, which is exclusively designed for and by Him to be a well for His eternal power and divine nature. Deep within the waters of this well resides an unexplainable longing for Him and the things of him, and from it gushes the knowledge of Him even if in the most basic terms.

The idea of the God-shaped hole is not only supported by Scripture, but it also supports the school of thought that even people living in the most remote parts of the earth will know of God at His pleasure. When He is ready to enter into a personal relationship with His creation, he will trouble the waters of that well. At that point, we will seek Him with all that we have, or we will try to fill the hole with something that does not fit.

Seeking him constantly with our whole mind, body, heart, and soul might give some cause for pause because it sounds overwhelming, daunting, or terrifying. Some might secretly fear that this might take away some of our 'goodies' and leave us with little time to worship our own desires.

However, if we choose to try to fill the hole with something else—anything else, whatever that 'thing' is, it will be consumed while it is—at the same time—consuming us. This would render us effectively inefficient, constrained by darkness, and in a vicious cycle of destitution and bondage.

While the latter is unsustainable as it will inevitably strain our system, and cause considerable drain, the former is a far better proposition because it not only awakens hope, but it also gives us passionate power, positive light, and perpetual liberation.

What is in a Name?

Our family home, circa 1972, was not energy efficient. There was no central air; we went through several refrigerators, each with a freezer either on top or on the side; and in addition, it was necessary that we kept a stand-alone, deep freezer in the basement that housed my daddy's many hunting treasures and meat purchases. Over time, this caused a strain on the antiquated wiring grid in the house.

Though he was a very handy man in his own right, daddy decided to call in a professional to assess the wiring situation in our home and to provide him an estimate of what it would cost to update, where needed, the electrical wiring to address the threat of our ever-evolving power dependency. Here, then, enters a nice White gentleman, dressed in a pair of khaki Dockers, a plaid workman's shirt, tan work boots, and carrying a litany of tools and instruments.

Daddy meets the man at the front door, shakes his hand, and escorts him to an electrical meter and fuse box, which was located on the kitchen wall, opposite the back door. After they chit-chatted for a while, daddy left the man to his own devices—to do his assessments and went out to the back room to puff on his pipe. That left me, a nosy 10-year-old, to spy on this man to make sure that he was doing what he was supposed to be doing and not dipping his hands in the cookie jar, so to speak.

So, there I stood, lurking behind the door that separated the kitchen from the dining room, peeking through the cracks and spying on this guy. And, just as the gentleman ran back down to the basement to take a look at what was going on down there, daddy, having finished his smoke, came back into the kitchen. Then, I, like the informant that I thought I was, popped into the kitchen to field any questions that daddy might have.

"Aw shucks!" daddy said. "I forgot that fella's name". Daddy did not want to appear impolite whenever the man reappeared for further discussion. Being the self-professed double agent that I was, I said, "Oh, you can call him Charlie". "Charlie? His name is Charlie?" daddy asked quizzically. "How do you know that?" To what I imagine was his total amazement, I responded, "Oh, I don't know; that's just what you call a White man when you don't know his name." Knowing his personality, I can bet daddy was tickled at my response, but he held a straight face and scolded, "Girl, you don't know what you're talking about...", and further demanded, "don't you call that man Charlie if that's not his name!" "Okay, I was just trying to help." Exit left.

Each Called by Name

Every appliance in a well-equipped kitchen has its own label and function, but aggregated, they are part of the kitchen system or apparatus. Each, individually, requires a capacity of power to perform as and when needed. In addition, they work best together to power and strengthen the function of the kitchen if they are aligned in such a way that by their placement, they support the work of the cook and the aesthetics of the room. I find the similarities of this to the synergies, functions, attributes of the God-head remarkable.

When Elohim (el-oh-heem): God "Creator, Mighty and Strong" formed man from the dust of the earth, and breathed into him life, he gave man a soul—a receptive place; a synergistic center; a place of power and strength.

He carved out that place in man's innermost being and sized it especially for His Spirit to dwell.

When Emmanuel (God With Us) came forth to walk with man, his purpose was to make a once-in-a-lifetime special delivery for all who would receive Him, that would mend and renew the special relationship between the Father and His creation.

When El-Shaddai (Almighty God Who Nourishes) looked over the desperation of his creation and saw the need, he at the appointed time, introduced himself through a Comforter and invited his sons and daughters to walk alongside him to be made perfect and prosper—not by might or strength, but by his power.

In short, God is truly an awesome God. And, while he has multiple names (or labels) with each representing a different attribute, he powers them all with His same essence.

Tips and Tricks for Kitchen Design

About Energy Efficient Appliances

According to the website www.energy.gov , homeowners can save energy and dollars through more efficient use of major kitchen appliances. Following are a few things of which we should be aware when thinking about replacing these appliances.

Consider purchasing appliances with blue EnergyStar® Label.

Refrigerator. Models with top-mounted freezers use 10%-25% less energy than side-by-side or bottom-mount units and are therefore more energy efficient.

Oven/Range. Consider a natural gas oven or range with automatic, electric ignition system. This saves gas since a pilot light is not burning continuously.

Dishwasher. Dishwashers purchased before 1994 use more than 10 gallons of water per cycle. Energy is required to heat the water. Consider a newer model which are required to use only 4.25 gallons of water per cycle.

Chapter 4

"Finally, brothers and sisters, whatever is true, whatever is noble, whatever is right, whatever is pure, whatever is lovely, whatever is admirable—if anything is excellent or praiseworthy—think about such things."
~ Philippians 4:8

The Pantry

Oh, the joy of the kitchen pantry.

In most kitchens, the pantry is a built-in storage space where small appliances might slip into obscurity, sometimes rendering them hard to reach. It is where spices and other small items might fade away from sight, found only after, in a fit of desperation and at a time of need, we run to the grocer and bring home from the store its replacement.

However, in some instances, it is a beautifully organized treasure-trove of goodies that helps make a little simpler the mundane tasks of life.

Then sometimes it is a place where your third oldest brother (as a youngster) hides out to play with matches, and then inadvertently starts a fire. However, so as not to cause him any further embarrassment about the latter, I digress.

The pantry stocks the kitchen and is, therefore, much like our mind, which interacts with the soul. Moreover, like the pantry, sometimes we find our minds cluttered with stuff where circumstances and situations might become too burdensome to bear, rendering us feeling helpless, desperate, and bogged down, or anxious about the hope of a prosperous life.

It might become a place where small things or precious moments might slip away; buried, and lost in the midst, and forever remembered only as missed opportunities or lost causes.

Sometimes, and ideally, it is a well-organized piece of the whole design; trained and disciplined on thinking only about those things that are noble, right, pure, lovely, admirable, excellent, or praiseworthy[10].

Yet, at its worst, it is sometimes a dark, lonely, hotbox where circumstances or someone somewhere, accidentally starts a fire of destruction.

The main thing our kitchen pantry and our mind might have in common is the need to be stocked and ready with supplements and items for nourishment and enrichment.

When stocking the pantry, the selections are straightforward and many because providing nourishment to the body by most is accomplished with liberty and sometimes reckless abandonment. However, feeding the body should cause us more thought and deliberation because our body is the temple and dwelling place of the Spirit of God the Most High. Additionally, speaking about the value of natural nutrition, Socrates advised, "Let your food be your medicine and your medicine be your food". Yet, even then, because of God's care, goodness, provision, and grace, we have what seems like an unlimited variety from which to choose and from many of those we happily make our selections.

As for what it takes for stocking the mind: if idle hands are the devil's workshop and idle lips are his mouthpiece; then without attempting to add to that already written, would not it follow that an idle mind might well be his Petri dish—where he tests and cooks up his schemes?

Since a well-stocked mind, which intercourses with the healthy soul, strengthens not only our body but also empowers us in our walk to be steadfast, unmovable, always abounding, while assuring us that our labor in Him is not in vain[11], shouldn't we be as diligent about feeding it as we are about feeding the body?

Unlike the accoutrements required for feeding the body, the variety of those things needed to fuel the mind are powerful yet few. While in no ways an all-inclusive list, they might include a constant intake of the Bread of

Life[12], the refreshing of Living Water[13], and daily (and nightly) portions Fruit of the vine[14].

Bread of Life

We grew up in a household of modest means. Though dad worked hard to provide for the family, mom in later years would recall the times when she owned only one or two dresses that she rotated for daily wear, while going about raising a caboodle of kids and making a home. She laughed about how she struggled to keep the dresses clean so that she could always have a clean one to wear to church on Sunday. Yet, despite this, I never remember our home ever being without sufficient vittles to feed the herd of us.

I often tease my older siblings, who married and left the nest when I was still young; saying that by the time that I came along, the family was living the life of the rich and famous. The factors that assisted these assertions were the facts that mom and dad were older and more established in their finances, and societal norms and circumstances had changed a bit.

I teased that while they might have grubbed on beans, Spam, and white bread when they were home, I grew up feasting on champagne and caviar.

That could not be farther from the truth; however, what is funny is that I must constantly reassure them that those stories are no more than tantalizing, made-up, myth.

I am thankful that at least for the better of my childhood years, we were somewhat fortunate as a family. This became obvious after realizing that although we prepared and ate fried bread, mustard, or sugar sandwiches because we liked them; some

> "They exchanged the truth of God for a lie, and worshiped and served created things rather than the Creator, who is forever worthy of praise! Amen"
>
> ~ ROMANS 1:25

did so because that was all they had. Bread was a household staple. A home that did not have anything else probably had at least a loaf of day-old bread. However, with the surge of the gluten-free trend and products on the market, it seems that real bread is losing its popularity.

I am not trying to discount the fact that some people are truly intolerant of and cannot digest some wheat products, which motivates them to replace those products with a viable alternative; that is a field of knowledge, which I lack enough understanding for which to speak. However, as I continue to observe and make correlations between the natural and the supernatural, it just seems even spiritually, some are slowly exchanging the Bread of Life for things that are trending and tempting, but far less filling. It is like exchanging what is real, natural, and pure for staged, distorted, or manufactured poison.

True to his humanitarian worldview, Mahatma Gandhi once said, "God comes to the hungry in the form of food". It is interesting for a variety of reasons how Gandhi, in that quote, touched upon not only the material need and moral duty of man, but also the need of the soul and the awesome provision of God. If we visit most any thriving, large city, we are likely to find the footways inundated with men, women, and sometimes children, holding signs telling of their desperate condition and begging alms. From a strictly humanitarian standpoint, we might grab a dollar or two, or a few coins from our pocket, toss it in their cup, receive a "God bless you", from them, and then go on about our business feeling good about our menial contribution. On the other hand, we might find ourselves stunned by how repulsed we might feel after experiencing an entire city block lined with the similar situations.

"Then he will say to those on his left, 'Depart from me, you who are cursed, into the eternal fire prepared for the devil and his angels. For I was hungry and you gave me nothing to eat, I was thirsty and you gave me nothing to drink, I was a stranger and you did not invite me in, I needed clothes and you did not clothe me. I was sick and in prison and you did not look after me.' They also will answer, 'Lord, when did we see you hungry or thirsty or a stranger or needing clothes or sick or in prison, and did not help you?'" He will reply, "Truly I will tell you, whatever you did not do for the least of these, you did not do for me."

~ MATTHEW 25:44-45

I recently visited one of those thriving cities. Although I kept a few extra dollars handy to respond to some of the needs, I also experienced the latter. I started feeling repulsed by the sheer number of panhandlers that I encountered, and all I wanted to do is escape it all, go back to my hotel room, bolt the door, and watch television. However, it was not quite so easy because the discourse that resulted on the inside was spectacular, yet also comforting.

I have engaged in enough Bible studies to consider how displeased Jesus is with those who do not help "the least of those" around us. In fact, he takes it personally. When my humanity wrestled with my 'sensibilities', I had to come to terms with understanding, and, naturally, I was losing the argument until the Spirit of God consoled my soul by bringing some things to my remembrance and feeding me more of the truth of his word. Searching my

> "Silver or gold I do not have, but what I do have I give you. In the name of Jesus Christ of Nazareth, walk."
>
> ~ ACTS 3:6

remorseful soul helped me to realize that the needy people and their plight did not repulse me; rather I was angry to see so many of them needing help. I realized that I was overwhelmed because of my desire to help, and despondent because I knew that I had to choose those whom to help and ignore the others. I could not help them all. Then by His grace, I remembered and considered the lame man's encounter with Peter and John and considered their response.

I have since come to terms with the fact that I am not able to save the world; that is not my job. In fact, whenever I pray for the needy who are out on the streets, I ask God to put in my path, those whom I am supposed to help and then I listen for that small still voice. I do not know if I always get it right, but I feel in my soul, the better for trying.

I have resolved to consider that maybe our humanitarian duty is to act on behalf of God and provide the help that we can when we can. However, our Christian charge is to intercede on behalf of the needy by praying for every soul we encounter and offer them, like Peter neither silver nor gold but a bite of the life-sustaining word of God and true Bread of Life. I am willing to suppose that in doing this, God will be pleased.

Living Water

Nothing puts a laugh in our bellies as adults than recalling daddy sitting not five feet from the kitchen yet calling us from upstairs or from way down the street to come and bring him a cold glass of water. What?! Not many things puzzled or annoyed us more. Yes, and when daddy said, "cold water", he meant cold water; not something he would otherwise characterize as "mule piss".

Daddy was a bit colorful with some of his usage of words or depictions of things. However, one thing that he was clear about was his role in the family as head of household and provider for his family. No one can rightfully say that, laziness prevented him from walking the few steps to the kitchen to get his own water; I believe it was more of his affirming the privilege for which he worked so hard and deserved.

History chronicles how asking for a drink of water can prove to be a small thing with big implications. For some, it led to establishing an important relationship as with Rebecca and Isaac[15]. For some, it preceded a righteous demise as with the courageous woman in the tent[16]. Moreover, for all, it reveals a truth that can change and save a life like the Samaritan woman at the well[17].

Water is the fuel of life both physically and spiritually. Naturally, its chemical make-up and compatibility to our anatomy makes it vital for the wellbeing of our mind and body. We can survive longer without food than without a good clean source of water.

Spiritually, it represents a purifying agent that cleanses and refreshes the soul. It also represents salvation and eternal life, which is the satisfying embodiment of the person of Jesus.

"...whoever drinks the water I give them will never thirst. Indeed, the water I give them will become a spring of water welling up to eternal life"

~ JOHN 4:14

One Tree, Many Fruit

Up the path and on the right side of the long gravel driveway that spanned the distance from the main street at the front of the house, to the standalone, two-car garage buried deep in the backyard, stood a very generous Vicar of Winkfield pear tree. It is not confirmed whether the tree was really of the species; however, the attributes of the tree and the fruit that it yielded seem to match up with the description of such.

The tree was vigorous and fruitful, and it stood strong, mighty, and prosperous for a long time. When time came for it to drop its fruit, we ended up with abundance.

The tree was unguarded in the yard, so neighbors were also welcomed to drop in to pick up a few. Ultimately, momma made pear preserves and canned as many jars as she could, to store away in the pantry for months of enjoyment.

I do not recall that we took any special care of the tree; it seemed to survive in its ecosystem fine. Simply nurtured by nature, the tree continued to bring forth its fruit in its season until it stopped. The same can be said about the blackberry and mulberry trees that we had as well, even though they were not as popular as the pear tree.

Each of the trees produced only one kind of fruit. The pear tree produced firm, delicious pears; the blackberry tree produced pithy, sweet, juicy blackberries; and the mulberry tree produced messy, tart mulberries, just as expected.

However, I recently learned that there is a tree in existence that produces more than one kind of fruit. For instance, this tree might produce peaches in one season, plums in the next, and apricots in another.

This is not a natural process but is, instead, due to a fabricated process of grafting branches from one type of fruit tree onto the base of a similar type of tree. Yet, while very crafty, this is not an original concept. Moreover, the correlation here of the natural to the supernatural is remarkable because Scripture also speaks of a divinely engineered tree that possesses this same feature as well.

The divinely engineered tree is the tree of life like one planted by rivers of water. It is blessed, and endowed with multiple fruit, where each blossom at its own time and in its own season[18]. The branches are the people of God.

The Master Designer grafts the faithful believers as wild branches onto the branches of the stable, deeply rooted, nourished tree. These branches have the benefit of growing and becoming prosperous by feeding from the sap of the tree, which is the source and the leaves, which is the word of God.

Each day the branches will yield a crop of fruit such as hopeful love, hilarious joy, reassured peace, courageous forbearance, discreet kindness, gracious goodness, faultless faithfulness, tender gentleness, and sacrificial self-control. By these we are preserved and blessed.

"Therefore, let us stop passing judgment on one another. Instead, make up your mind not to put any stumbling block or obstacle in the way of a brother or sister."

~ ROMANS 14:13

The Legend of the Vicar

Years passed and I do not recall exactly what happened to the pear tree. Maybe a storm toppled it, as it was dying its own death. I do, however, recall that it went from being a big tree, tall and mighty, to being a little, short stump that hosted an annoying colony of hungry, fiery ants.

In its diminished and unproductive state, it became a nuisance and the source of mischief and mishaps. Rather than being a place that provided refreshment and shade from the sun, it became a stumbling block[19] where we suffered many scrapes and bruises while playing kickball and catch. In addition, if that were not bad enough, whenever daddy decided to remove the stump by setting it afire, it became the place where my niece learned a terrible lesson about throwing gasoline on fire. Thank God that but for a few serious burns and bruises to her legs, she survived fine.

Even so, even as the tree ceased to exist, the bounty of its fruit—preserved and tucked away in our pantry—continued to supplement and provide for our nourishment for many years to come, and we were blessed.

Tips and Tricks for Kitchen Design

Ideas for Organizing the Pantry

A well-organized pantry is not only a chef's dream but is also helpful for saving the few dollars we would otherwise spend to repurchase items already on hand but buried by clutter. Organize the pantry by considering one or a combination of the following tips.

- Use and over-the-door organizer to add additional storage for quick-reach items.
- Group food items and place in labeled storage bins.
- Flip wire shelves so that the lip is on top and use to store can goods on their sides, rather than upright.
- Create pull-out storage area at the bottom to house small appliances.
- Use over-the-door, multi-pair, shoe pockets to hold jars of condiments, sauces, etc.
- Remove stationary shelving, install pegboard on walls, organize and store items in hanging baskets; and finally,
- Make organizing the pantry a priority.

Chapter 5

"...I have learned the secret of being content in any and every
situation, whether well-fed or hungry, whether living in plenty or in
want. I can do all things through
him who give me strength." ~Phi-
lippians 4:12-13

Spice of Abundant Life

As I said, daddy was a good cook, and he did some interesting things in the kitchen. Nevertheless, I think we considered him more of a provider than a chef. Momma, on the other hand, really knew how to put things together. I learned a lot about cooking just by watching her in the kitchen.

Even though she was what some would call an old-time, southern cook, momma was very sophisticated about measuring and adding ingredients, but only when necessary. I learned the best lessons about seasoning food by watching her looking down over a pot of greens, stirring a pan of cornbread dressing, or powdering chicken to get it ready for the fryer. She instinctively knew when enough was enough.

T. T. CAROLE

Unlike the popular chefs that we see featured on the popular lot of reality shows today who taste as they go along, momma would season, and when she was finished, she would invite others to taste. She would then ask, "Does it need anything else; maybe a little more pepper?" If the answer was yes, it was only at her suggestion.

Both momma and daddy knew their way around the kitchen and each instinctively understood the "science of cooking". They were "old school". They knew how to stretch a meal in leaner times and share when there was abundance. However, whether seasoning food in the kitchen or peppering us with their faith, they knew what they knew, did their best that they could do, and trusted God for the rest.

The Science of Salt

Salt is not a spice; it is a mineral, and an especially important and valuable one, at that. Few will dismiss its importance naturally or figuratively whether in the spice rack or in the prudence and providence of God.

After doing a study and consulting several online resources, I came to better understand the significance and value of salt. While what I share here is not exhaustive, the breadth of what I discovered is amazing.

The importance, complexities, and uses of salt are known and evident, even dating back thousands of years, to Antiquity. For the ancients, the symbolism and benefits made salt significant and gave credence to its value. In fact, salt

> "Salt is good, but if it loses its saltiness, how can you make it salty again? Have salt among yourselves, and be at peace with each other,"
>
> ~ MARK 9:50

was so valuable a commodity that depending on the circumstances, some ancients hoarded it; some used it for barter or trading; some presented it as offering in their religious ceremonies; and like us, most used it for flavoring their food.

In addition, salt, in its natural state, served as an antiseptic for healing the sick; a preservative for protecting a food supply; and as a purifier for cleansing the water for bathing the precious newborn babies. One interesting thing about the latter is that if salt were not readily available for the baby's bath water, the attendant would, in its stead, wash the baby in donkey's urine. That said, I am neither judging nor making this up.

Emblematically for the ancients, and maybe for some today, the presence of salt (whether in meals, religion, or rituals), symbolizes and represents friendship, spiritual health and vigor, holiness, hospitality, fidelity, purity and a covenant between God and his people. In addition, as evidenced by the fate of Lot's wife, it sorely represented punishment for an act of disobedience[20].

There is much discourse about how we use and consume salt today. We could probably agree about the soothing and somewhat healing effect of a warm, salted, scented bath. We could probably also agree about how well it enhances the taste of our food. Moreover, if we paid any attention, we could probably agree that the fluids in our body need salt in order to keep our cells functioning properly. The debate, therefore, is usually not about whether we should use it, or not, but rather about how much of it we should use.

We grew up on a song, that we enjoyed singing in church that goes:

"We are the salt of the earth; our bright light shining in a very dark world. While he has gone to prepare us a place, we are the salt of the earth. We must stand up when others sit down; we must smile when others frown. Some people find that it is so hard to do. It is all left up to me and you."

Though I am not sure who wrote, sang, or produced the original version, I do know that John P. Kee and Rance Allen are credited with the modern-day version.

The song is based on Jesus' instructions to his followers about what should 'be the attitudes' of those who are working or striving for the rewards of the Kingdom of Heaven.

After his instruction, Jesus warns that if we who are striving for the rewards do not keep ourselves refreshed and immersed in the holiness of his covenant, then we become ineffective at best and maybe even useless and cast out at worst.

This might prove salt a particularly important staple in our kitchen as part of our soul food because, metaphorically, the benefits have proved to be many, in that it preserves us, heal us, cleanses us, guide us and bond us together with Him in His covenant. If we keep our rack right, our souls will be good and salty.

The Healing Power of Honey

Oh, how we would love to go to Soulard Market. Every other Saturday morning, my parents would load those of us who wanted to go, into the car and we would head out to Soulard Market. The trip was probably a 15-20-minute drive from home, but when you are a kid riding in the back of a car and heading for what, in your mind, is your next big adventure, every trip seems like a trip of a thousand miles.

We would make it to the parking lot, search out a parking spot, then finally go into the market and watch momma negotiate with the men and women selling their produce. She always looked for the stands with the nicest looking fruits and vegetables. Whenever she spotted one, she would go over and ask for whatever poundage she was looking to buy. However, she was always suspicious of some of the vendors who liked to pack her bag from the back of the pile. She feared that they would use a slight of hand and not pack their best. "Take them from the front", she would tell them. Some of the vendors might not have liked it but they usually did just as she demanded.

Those trips to the market were somewhat educational because it seems we would gain exposure to some very fascinating sights, sounds, tastes, and experiences. My parents were always as generous with us as they could afford to be. Because of this, we did not just walk away from the market with fruits, eggs, vegetables, and other essentials. Sometimes we got pet birds, and sometimes we scored some interesting and very tasty snacks.

However, sometimes we just got a pat on the head from a local politician who was running for office.

We were a large family to feed and were in no way spoiled kids. Therefore, whenever momma and daddy splurged on those extras, it was for good reason.

One of our all-time favorites, which is not only considered a snack but also a food, was the packaged honeycomb square. It was so cool to be able to eat the product in its natural state either as a sweet, sticky treat that we licked off our fingers, or

> "Eat honey ...for it is good: honey from the comb is sweet to your taste. Know also that wisdom is like honey for you: if you find it, there is a future for you, and your hope will not be cut off."
>
> ~ PROVERBS 24:13, 14

atop of some buttered, home-made biscuits for a delightfully filling and satisfying meal.

I would like to believe that momma and daddy, in their own way, allowed us to indulge in those little pleasures as a way of permitting themselves to remain curious about things as well. On the other hand, they were rooted and grounded in the word of God and were aware of the mention of the medicinal qualities of honey in the scriptures. For this particular treat, they, in the back of their minds, might have been remembering how the word likens honey to the wisdom, word, and essence of God and it says that honey is a necessity and is good and edifying for the soul.

Leaven: Friend or Foe

While I admired some of the work of the late, great Maya Angelou as a youth, I did not fully come to appreciate the depth of her understanding or the breadth of her wisdom until I reached maturity and got over 'being young'. However, judging by the far-reaching expressions in her book, "Wouldn't Take Nothing for My Journey Now", where she demonstrates her own dealing with, and growing past the various "isms" that might visit us all at some point in life, I somehow think she would applaud and appreciate the tenaciousness of my youth.

Ms. Angelou, not unlike many prolific writers, seemed to write from a place of earned learning, lessons bought, teachings taught, and gracious gratitude, all while celebrating her 'now' station in life. This is a place where we should all be so lucky as to discover for ourselves as life progresses. It is a place of confidence, contentment, and conviction, which is a resting place for the soul.

When we are in this place of contentment or simply striving for it, we position ourselves to experience and enjoy the dynamic, unfolding events that life has to offer in new, satisfying, and instructive ways. That kind of contentment keeps us from becoming complacent in how we value each experience. Dr. Seuss said it this way: "Sometimes you will never know the value of a moment until it becomes a memory". It is good to have and value great memories of a beautiful life once lived and its many experiences—warts and all. They not only provide food for life; they are also the makings great stories.

Emblazoned in my mind continues to be memories of growing up in a lower to middle class African American community where my friends and civic trends were richly entrenched in the Black Experience. Each experience encompassed the traditions to which we adhered, the ideas we expressed, the clothes we wore, the words we spoke, and importantly, the food we ate. This was 'home'.

Though always curious, I was not able to discover additional new and exciting things until I left the safe and familiar shelter of 'home'. The new and exciting things in turn, created some exciting new memories, stories, and 'ah ha' moments, yet many of those bring me back to home.

"Your boasting is not good. Don't you know a little yeast leavens the whole batch of dough? Get rid of the old yeast, so that you may be a new unleavened batch—as you really are. For Christ, our Passover lamb, has been sacrificed. There-fore, let us [celebrate], not with the old bread leavened with malice and wickedness, but with the unleavened bread of sincerity and truth."

~ 1 CORINTHIANS 5:6-8

As I continue to ruminate over momma's soul food cooking skill or daddy's edginess, I must say that we enjoyed a variety of meals from the kitchen. It was not unlike momma to whip up some corned beef and cabbage for St. Pat-rick's Day, or Rumaki to go along with dinner. She also cooked a lot of homemade breads, cakes, and rolls; however, I do not recall her partici-pating in the fad of making and sharing the Herman cake or Amish friendship bread.

In either case the Herman cake or the Amish friendship bread, starts with a small portion of a batter made from flour, milk, sugar, warm water, and yeast (the catalyst), which the owner feeds and nurtures for several days, or in some cases, weeks. The Ancients called this batter leaven.

In the end, the ingredients grow and become so potent over that period that the owner divides the batter into several portions during final preparation: one to make into the bread (or cake) and bake, one to keep for starting over, and two portions to share with a couple of friends.

As I said, I did not know of this from my parents' kitchen. It was not until after leaving the shelter of home and meeting people outside of my immediate sphere of influence that this was introduced into my experience.

When we leave the comfort and shelter of home, we might meet and learn valuable lessons about many things that we might find new, different, and exciting. While we might long for the experience of nurturing, feeding, and sharing some of those things, which in the end might prove to be good, it is good to discern when it is best to leave some things alone.

I learned that the driver of the whole process of making, growing, sharing, and even preserving the batter (or leaven) for Hermann cake or Amish friendship bread is the proper handling of the yeast, which is a powerful organism. After the batter is sufficiently yeasted it, at best, will cause the bread or cake rise into a beautiful, delicious treat that we are happy to share. However, at worst, if not handled properly, the yeasted batter will puff up for a time, only to sink into a flattened mess.

Similarly, where the batter (or leaven) represents what is good for the soul, at best the end-product is pleasant and profitable and promotes good works; however, at worst, it might represent things that we unintentionally hold on to and continue to feed, nurture and eventually, because the situations might become bigger than imagined, we share in error. Some of the things that we might feed unnecessarily might be a hurt that we sustained at the hands of another; it might be a loss of a loved one or a self-inflicted wound; or it might be mistrust, distrust, uncertainty, or disobedience. Whatever it is, is bound to sink us into a mass of hopelessness and despair.

In any case, the effects of the batter (or leaven) are powerful and persistent. However, in the end, it is not bad for the soul, as long as we prayerfully get rid of any batch that is bad from the start and carefully only nurture the one that promotes good and Godly results.

Tips and Tricks for Kitchen Design

Herman or Friendship Bread Starter & Cake

Starter:

1 package dry yeast

½ cup warm (105 degrees) water (to activate yeast)

2 teaspoons sugar

2 ½ cups all-purpose flour

2 cups warm water

Mix yeast, ½ cup water and sugar. When yeast is foamy, stir in flour and additional water. Place in large crock or glass jar. Cover with damp cloth and rubber band. (Do not use a metal container.) Keep at room temperature for five days, stirring daily with a WOODEN SPOON (important).

After five days, feed Herman 1 cup flour, 1 cup milk, ¾ cup sugar. Keep covered under damp towel at room temperature. Stir daily.

On the tenth day, feed Herman 1 cup flour, 1 cup milk, ¾ cup sugar.

Herman is now ready to be divided up and baked. Use 2 cups for baking. Save 1 cup, and continue feeding, on the fifth and tenth days for 10 more days (when he will be ready to bake again) and give 2 cups to friends (along with these instructions) to grow.

Herman Friendship Cake:
2 cups Herman
2 cups flour
3 eggs
2/3 cup light salad oil
½ tsp. salt
1 tsp. baking soda
2 tsps. baking powder
1 ½ tsps. cinnamon
1 cup sugar
1 tsp. nutmeg
1 tsp ginger
Optional Ingredients: Raisins, apples, dried apricots, carrots, zucchini, walnuts, pecans,
Preheat oven to 350 degrees. Generously grease a 12-cup Bundt or tube pan. Mix all ingredients together until smooth, adding 2 cups of desired, optional ingredients to batter. Bake 1 hour. Remove from pan and cool on rack. Serve at room temperature.
Do not forget to share.

Chapter 6

"The law of the LORD is perfect, refreshing the soul. The statutes of the LORD are trustworthy, making wise the simple." ~ Psalm 19:7

The Essential Kitchen Tools

When we think about the essential tools needed to add simplicity for the cook and tastiness to a meal in the kitchen, we could probably come up with quite a few. However, thinking about that from the point of view of someone who grew up in a home of good southern, soul food cooks, then the one thing on the top of the list would probably be the cast iron skillet.

> "And Jesus answered him, saying, It is written, that man shall not live by bread alone, but by every word of God."
>
> ~ LUKE 4:4

Of course, the cast iron skillet is big and heavy and does little to add simplicity for the cook, but it helps to work wonders with a skillet of fried chicken.

Some might say that a measuring cup (whether an actual measuring cup or an eight-ounce drinking cup) is required in order to get that proper proportionate mix of flour to cornmeal for making that delicious, perfectly cratered, and crusty, golden brown skillet of cornbread.

Then some might remember that great big butcher's knife, used for cutting up chicken, fileting fish, or chopping other meats into their individual portions.

Finally, some might have a flashback about a big pot of mixed greens, black-eyed peas, butter, lima, or great white northern beans that was so delicious that none of remaining pot liquor was poured down the drain, but rather was sopped up with a sliver of cornbread until it was no more. That might bring to their mind the need for the long-handled spoon, used to keep those pots stirred.

There were many other vessels and apparatuses needed and used in the kitchen as well. However, whenever we give our thoughts permission to linger on those food items that not only tasted good but also remind us of the comforts of home, then it is acceptable that we pay not as much attention to detail as we do to the final product. In the end, comfort food was always the result of all of the appliances and gadgets.

I recently learned from Wikipedia that the term 'comfort food' can be traced back to around 1966 when it was first used in a news article that was focusing on the positive, psychological affect certain foods had on adults who were in the midst of life-changing or stressful situations.

For the adult subjects of the study, researchers found that comfort food, or food that reminded those of better or simpler times, helped them to cope and find comfort and hope when things are going a little rough. Somehow finding their way back to being a child, chowing down on a favorite food at momma's table, or maybe enjoying a coveted treat while watching baseball with daddy, assured them that things are not as bad as they seemed.

However, there are times, though, when it feels like we are slipping into a desperate and lonely place, and we feel grieved and famished deep in our souls. We feel like the very soul where we go to for nourishment is dried up and despondent. And, in those times, the enemy will seize every moment that we are there to offer us something that is neither palatable nor worthy of our time, talent, or attention. Those are the times when thinking nostalgically about momma's magical cooking or daddy's special treats are not going to give us any comfort. Food to feed our physical bodies is not enough; we need the kind of comfort that cannot be bought or made. Yet there is hope.

If a kitchen was falling apart, and we have the means, we would strip it down to its foundation and rebuild it to our satisfaction. Like that, it is essential that during those

"I waited patiently for the LORD; and he turned to me and heard my cry. He lifted me out of the slimy pit, out of the mud and mire; he set my feet on a rock and gave me a firm place to stand.

~ PSALM 40: 1, 2

times when our heart is heavy and feeling overwhelmed, we go to He who rebuilds and comforts us in all our troubles, to refresh our soul by stripping away the muck and mire that has us bound and restore us into illustrious relationship to Him.

The Vessel: Blessed and Set Apart

Do we all have a dish or two that even though it is multi-functional—as most are—we are convinced and satisfied to use it for a single, special purpose? Up until a few years ago, I had a ceramic pot that became that for me.

The pot was simply beautiful. It was made of clay and shaped like an old-fashioned kettle or little potbelly stove. It had handles at the top on each side that would put into your mind the image of a fat and happy, country cook standing with her arms at her sides, bent at the elbows, with her hands placed squarely, high up on her waist. Its color on

> "But the pot he was shaping from the clay was marred in his hands: so the potter formed it into another pot, shaping it as seemed best to him."
>
> ~ JEREMIAH 18:4

the outside was like that of the darkest red kidney bean, highly glazed with a couple of layers of shellac. The inside, color looked of fired clay. The lid, which fit neatly on top, had a little topknot-like pull for ease of handling, and that further lent itself to the look of the happy cook.

This pot would have worked well for the preparation of any number of dishes, but to me, it begged for cooking chili. In fact, every time I ran across it in the cabinet, I was suddenly in the mood to do just that, cook chili.

Over time, with use, and due to some gentle abuse, my favorite chili pot started falling apart. First, it lost one handle, then the other. Finally, the lid crashed to the floor and shattered into many pieces.

The pot served me well through countless servings of homemade chili; however, it became unusable in its current state. Yet, I did not have the heart to throw it out so, instead, I drilled a few holes into the base for drainage and repurposed the chili pot into a flower container, filled with an array of fragrant and delicious herbs.

Much like that, when we are in Christ, our soul operates in an esteemed place, which is securely enshrined in the hands of our Lord and Maker. However, sometimes even while there—there is evidence of bruising and pain. Pressures of outside sources sometimes are the cause and sometimes the cause is the Lord's corrective actions because of the tension of our operating outside of his will.

Whichever is the case: whether we are bruised and broken because of sin or because of correction, as long as our soul is anchored in Jesus and securely placed in loving and creative hands, we can be sure that He will cover our wounds or reconstruct our crushed selves to be whatever it is that He desires for us to be.

In each instance, after a treasured vessel was wounded and broken, each, though still flawed, were made over to be what its possessor wanted it to be.

The Measuring Cup

I recently ran across a fascinating parable about a wise, ole owl. Then, after the bright-eyed discovery and initial amazement over how relevant the story seems to situations at hand, I conducted additional research to test to what extent the parable is based on reality.

The parable, which is posited as "The Owl was God", was published in 1940, by James Thunder. In the parable, the other beasts in the field revered the owl because he appeared to possess skills and insight that they feared they were lacking.

This unique skillset was discovered by a couple of moles, who, under the dark covering of night, realized, to their amazement, that the owl could see them as they tried to sneak by. Upon being discovered, the moles quizzed the owl to test the veracity of his sight and wisdom. Upon doing this, they deemed him wise and above reproach. They were so satisfied with the results of the tests, that the moles presented their findings to others in the field, in hopes of crowning the owl their leader.

There was, however, a contingent among the group that posed additional questions concerning the owl's abilities. Accepting that the owl was untouchable under the covering of darkness (which was the case each time the moles approached him), a sly fox and a couple of his friends—maybe a poodle and a mouse—wanted to know if the owl could perform equally well in the daylight. To this question and untested, the majority of the creatures, answered with a roaring, "YES!" and they laughed hysterically at the small contingent and

> "We do not dare compare ourselves with some who commend themselves. When they measure themselves by themselves and compare themselves with themselves, they are not wise.
>
> ~ 2 CORINTHIANS 10:12

eventually drove them out of the forest. They then declared that the owl was god.

The owl, who was intimately familiar with his shortcoming, which was not immediately apparent to the others, accepted the invitation of the beasts of the fields to become their leader and in effect, their god. They wanted him to lead them, and at high noon, he did exactly that.

Early in many conventional theological or Bible studies, good students, after even a brief encounter with the breadth of God, will often learn in a hurry how much they really do not know. They will measure themselves by God Almighty and His standards and then realize just how small they are in comparison. Moreover, they will discover and attest to a well-rehearsed phrase often quoted by the learned and humble, which simply states, "There is only one God and I am not Him".

The parable hints at the falsely believed notion that owls are blind in the daylight. This is somewhat deceptive. Owls do have daylight vision; however, because of the makeup of their eyes (which enables their keen, 3-D, night vision), their extremely large pupils do not close to adjust to bright sunlight as do humans. Therefore, during the daylight, and especially in bright sun, they have to self-adjust by partially closing their eyes to filter it.

Even with their enormous eyes partially closed, they can see fine. However, the lids covering the top portion of their eyes restrict their vision, leaving them not able to see the sky above the lids; they only see what is in the areas down below.

Both, the humorous and the tragic parts of the parable demonstrate the danger of thinking more highly of oneself than one ought.[21]

To their excitement, the wise ole owl, with his obstructed vision, yet acting like god, ending up leading the gaggle of beast out of the confines of

> "yet for us there is but one God, the Father from whom all things came and for whom we live, and there is but one Lord, Jesus Christ, through whom all things cam and through whom we live."
>
> ~ 1 CORINTHIANS 8:5

the forest for their first excursion.

The most humorous thing to happen on this excursion is that on the way, the owl struggled and bumped into many objects that he could not see. Yet rather than confess his shortcoming; and rather than his followers question what seemed like his disabilities or their decision to follow his lead, like drunken minions, the beasts, too, would bump into those same objects because they believed that was the cool thing to do. The tragedy came, however, when as they followed the owl across a busy road. Like the wise ole owl that became god, most of them died when they were run over by a big, oncoming, truck.

The purported moral to Mr. Thunder's story is that "You can fool too many of the people too much of the time". However, I would like to bring it home and frame it as a reminder to trust in the one true God alone, because he is Perfect, and he alone, "...refreshes [our] soul [and] guides [us] along the right paths for his name's sake"[22].

The Knife and the Sword

What is a well-appointed kitchen without a knife; and what is a well-equipped soul without its sword?

The other day I truly got a kick out of one of my young nephews when I visited to drop off a package at his parents' house.

After a lengthy visit, as I was gathering my things, putting on a coat, and preparing to leave, I happened to glance into the kitchen where I got a glimpse of my young nephew, who was busy chopping hard, boiled eggs for the family's dinner salad.

> "The word of God is alive and active. Sharper than any double-edge sword, it penetrates even to dividing soul and spirit, joints and marrow; it judges the thoughts and attitudes of the heart.
>
> ~ HEBREWS 4:12

"Oh, my goodness; he is chopping eggs like a pro", I said in amazement. "Oh yeah, I taught him how to use the knife in that way", his dad said proudly. "Are you tucking those fingers?" I asked. "Yes, my fingers are tucked", he assured me with a great big smile. I continued to watch as he, almost expertly, glided the knife, and guided the eggs in unison.

This young lad is 12 years old, and he loves science and Legos. He has a small, thin frame, the brightest eyes, and the most adorable smile that you can imagine on a boy of that age. Because he was such a joy to watch, I guess I could not stop watching him, and he, wanting his skills on full display, could not stop cutting.

Then finally, "That's probably enough", his dad counseled. "Ok", he replied, seeming somewhat disappointed. He then used the knife to scoop up the chopped eggs into his hands and eventually sprinkled his masterfully chopped trimmings, high atop the bowl of mixed greens.

With his skills and hard work, I am quite sure that the salad was simply delicious.

This causes me to remember, too, the lessons daddy taught my siblings and I on how to use the knife in the kitchen. We were trained to use the knife to descale fish.

Whenever daddy would go fishing and bring back a load of fish, we would spread old newspaper over a table or even the floor of the back porch (because it was such a messy job), and then go to work.

"Go down near the tail and find where the scales are loose", he advised; "then push the knife away from you and towards the head". In addition, of course, he added, "Watch your fingers!" We did pretty well, and we eventually graduated to learning how to skin and gut fish as well.

The one thing that daddy did not teach us early on about dressing a fish, is how to debone it. Deboning is the process of separating the meat of the fish from its bone structure. This allows you to preserve the good stuff and purge all of the junk. It also requires a different kind of knife, and a greater level of skill and maturity that, even to this day; I have no desire to master.

Deboning is much like the process exercised in every soul after feeding on a steady diet of God's word, and with similar results: over time, and with maturity, our soul compels us to keep the good stuff and purge anything unbecoming.

We essentially change from the inside out. Lao Tzu, a Chinese philosopher, once said: "The soul has no secret that the behavior does not reveal".

Fed by the Long-handled Spoon

As an accessory to the décor of the kitchen of our family home included a gigantic, wooden spoon and fork set, which were in clear view, where they hung on display on a kitchen wall. As kids, we were always interested in the spoon and fork set; however, it is surprising that none of us, even jokingly, ever tried to use them to either eat or feed our siblings.

This reminds me of an enlightening story that is beloved by many religions and cultures but is owned by none and the author is unknown. To the best of my recollection, the story begins with a person simply asking the Lord, "Please show me the difference between heaven and hell". The Lord obliged by leading the tourist to a place where there were two rooms, each behind its own door.

The Lord opened the first door that represented hell and inside were many people who appeared miserable and gaunt. This, first, was a mystery to the tourist because they spotted, in the middle of the table, a pot of delicious smelling stew, and all the residents of the room were in possession of a long-handled spoon, long enough to dip into the pot. However, upon further examination, the tourist realized that though the spoons were long enough for them to dip them into the stew, they were also so long that the residents were not able to maneuver them back to their mouths to reap the rewards.

Next, the Lord opened the second door, which represented heaven. Right away, the tourist noticed that, in the center of the table, there was a pot of delicious smelling stew, and in the hand of each resident was a long-handled spoon, very much like the ones seen in the other room. The stunning, difference, however, was that all the residents in that room were joyful, fat, and happy.

Exasperated by this, the tourist then inquired of the Lord, saying, "Lord, I don't get it. Both rooms had in the center of its table a hearty, delicious-smelling pot of stew, for all to enjoy, and the residents in each possessed the same long-handled spoon. What is the difference? Why are the residents of the one room so miserable and starving to death and the ones in the other so fat and full of joy?"

The Lord answered the tourist and said, "The residents in the first room were stiff-necked, hard-headed, selfish, and too stubborn to acknowledge or rely upon anybody but themselves. They are dying needlessly while trying to figure things out." He continued, "When the residents of the second room realized that they could not feed themselves with their own long spoons, each decided to submit to one another, by sacrificing their own food, and focus on feeding the neighbor within reach of the spoon. By doing this, everybody benefitted from someone else's spoon, and they found joy in serving each other." Then the Lord asked, "Which would you choose?"

Tips and Tricks for Kitchen Design

Cousin Helen's San Diego Coleslaw

Ingredients:
1 large bag of coleslaw mix
1 bunch fresh celery (chopped)
3 cloves garlic (minced)
½ red bell pepper (chopped)
1 small red onion (chopped)
1 cup sugar
½ cup white distilled vinegar
½ cup water
½ cup cooking oil
A pinch of salt
Cayenne pepper (to taste)
Cajun seasoning (to taste)
Celery seeds (to taste)

Instructions:
Add all liquids and sugar to a pot and bring to a boil, stirring occasionally.

Rinse slaw and let drain.

Combine slaw mix, red bell pepper, celery, onion, and garlic in large, lidded container and toss.

When sugar is fully dissolved, pour hot liquid mixture over the slaw mix.

Stir in remaining ingredients to taste.

Cover and refrigerate overnight for best results.

Pour mixture into colander to drain liquids from slaw before serving.

Chapter 7

"How priceless is your unfailing love, O God! People take refuge in the shadow of your wings. They feast on the abundance of your house, you give them drink from your river of delights." ~ Psalm 36:7, 8

The Feast

A feast, like baptism, is an outward expression of an inward celebration. For the feast, the celebration usually centers around a praiseworthy feat, an act of grace or kindness, a milestone or major accomplishment, or liberation from a form of oppression. For baptism, the celebration singularly focuses on the life-changing event of being buried, resurrected, and living in freedom with our Savior.

At a feast, in addition to food-lined tables, there is usually music, song, and dance. At the baptism, heaven rejoices, the Lamb is the main course, and there is joy, unspeakable joy.

Whenever we leave the feast, we might feel too full to move. However, whenever we leave the baptism, we will feel more fully and will be compelled to move.

Each event requires preparation and sacrifice, and each has its own rewards.

An Inconvenient Truth

LOL (laughing out loud), SMH (shaking my head), IJS (I am just saying), BTW (by the way) and BFF (best friend forever). Those are just some of the many acronyms created and made popular in this revolutionary age of text messaging.

Though a convenient way to shorthand a message to get it out more quickly, acronyms can also leave you SYH (scratching your head), if you do not keep current on them. There is one, however, for which I searched but did not find on the massive list of the ones currently used. The acronym is 'FAT'.

I have had the great fortune of taking classes on lots of interesting

> "He told them, "The harvest is plentiful, but the workers are few. Ask the Lord of the harvest, therefore, to send out workers into his harvest field."
>
> ~ LUKE 10:2

subjects over the course of my life. Of all the disciplines that required great depth of thinking, I find that the deepest, most honest, and sometimes more challenging discourse happens in the midst of the theological discussions where the topic always turned to God.

The one thing that the different teachers who taught these classes had in common was that they did not openly argue or disagree with a point of view even if it were different from their own; they simply went to the word and challenged us to find Scriptural support for whatever argument we might have. Nevertheless, there is always that one teacher or incident that stands out.

This teacher, who, BTW, was also a particularly good teacher, was the one who came closest to accidently starting an unnecessary argument that was totally off subject.

Imagine walking into a classroom late and feeling rushed after a long day at work and then being stuck in traffic trying to make it there on time. Prior to that moment, while on the way there you remember you have half of a sandwich, some cold fries and a flat Pepsi left over from lunch, which you decided.

to woof down on the way to prevent the nag of hunger from rearing its ugly head during the 4-hour class. Then by the time you make it to your destination, you are feeling a little bloated and self-conscious as you step out of the car because it feels like your tummy is about to blow a button off the front of your blouse. Finally, you walk into the room and the next words you hear pouring out of the teacher's mouth are, "We should all be so FAT".

"Excuse me!" I shouted in my head.

By the time I scooted into the first seat I could grab, settle my books and bags on and around the table, and was about to protest to let my displeasure be known about the snide remark, he continued, "The harvest is plentiful and the labor is few. Therefore, the Bible tells us to pray with and for each other so that we can tend to his harvest. The Lord needs people who are F (faithful), A (available), and T (teachable)".

Well, okay then. That cleared that up nicely. Audibly this time, I said, "Preach, teacher!"

The teacher, by way of the word, hit the nail on the head; there is work to do in the kingdom for which we should be prepared. Therefore, like the delightful concept of momma's and daddy's well-stocked kitchen, the burden of the soul is to keep us FAT and happy while we prepare for the ultimate feast.

DISHING SOUL FOOD IN THE KITCHEN

A Prayer for the Feast

Abba Father, Father of Abraham, Isaac, and Jacob, and Father of my Lord and Savior, Jesus Christ. Father, there is none like you. You are the Maker, Creator, and Keeper of this great universe. You open your hand and feed nations. Your satisfying waters flow like a river.

Father, apart from you, I am a sinner undone. Please forgive my sins and hear my prayer.

I come to you as thirsty as a deer, panting for even a drop of water from your everlasting stream. My soul is aching, my heart is breaking, everything within me is starving for your attention. Yet I will praise you.

Father, my hope is in you, alone. By your power, please restore this, your broken vessel. Feed and refresh my soul with the bounty of your goodness. Protect me from further brokenness and any schemes of the enemy. Please bring back to my remembrance, as I pour out my soul, the joy of knowing your great love and care for me.

Let your waves and breakers sweep over me in the roar of your deep waterfalls, and LORD, continue to direct your love towards me all day as I sing songs of praise to you at night.

Father, my hope is in you, alone and I am happy to
suffer your good and all-knowing will.
LORD, I pray this prayer and ask these things by the
power of your Holy Spirit, and in the blessed name of Jesus the Christ. AMEN

(adapted from Psalms 42)

Tips and Tricks for Kitchen Design

The Art of Setting a Table

Whether you are setting up for a formal dinner for family and friends, an intimate meal for two, or just a quiet evening alone, the following tips will help to enhance the mood.

A beautifully set table, with or without a cloth, starts with a well-proportioned, beautifully placed centerpiece. It does not have to be elaborate; even a few fresh (or silk) flowers poking out of the tops of a good-looking wine bottle will do the trick. Surround that with a few candles, and you will be on your way.

Add a placemat to protect the surface.

For a bit of added elegance, center a charger plate, which is of a design that complements the dinner plate, on the placemat. Note: these may be left in place when all other dishes are removed after the dinner.

Place dinner plate, silverware, and beverage ware as follows:

- Set dinner plate atop charger.
- Add, soup bowl atop dinner plate (if needed).

- Working from left to right on the left side of the dinner plate, place a dinner fork, salad fork, then a folded napkin.
- Still working to the left of the plate, place a bread-and-butter plate above the forks and set a butter knife in its center.
- Above and centered to the dinner plate, place a dessert spoon or fork, or both (opposite facing).
- Working from left to right on the right side of the dinner plate, place the dinner knife, the teaspoon, then the soup spoon.
- Place the water glass above the dinner knife.
- Place a white wine glass to the right of the water glass. If red wine is also served, place a red wine glass slightly above and centered to the water goblet and the white wine glass.

All set and ready to enjoy.

ABOUT THE AUTHOR

T. T. Carole is a business professional and student of the Bible with formal training in both areas. She has a passion for encouraging others to become their personal best while nurturing their relationship with God and celebrating His spirt within.

Notes

---

[1] Jeremiah 20:9 (NIV) "…his word is in my heart like a fire, a fire shut up in my bones. I am weary of holding it in; indeed, I cannot.

[2] Philippians 2:12-13 (NIV) "Therefore, my dear friends, as you have always obeyed—not only in my presence, but now much more in my absence—continue to work out your salvation with fear and trembling, for it is God who works in you to will and to act in order to fulfill his good purpose."

[3] Philippians 2:13-13 (NIV) See above.

[4] Psalm 62.1 (NIV) "Truly my soul finds rest in God; my salvation comes from him."

[5] Matthew 7:7 (NIV) "Ask and it will be given to you; seek and you will find; knock and the door will be opened to you."

[6] Philippians 4:6 (NIV) "Do not be anxious about anything, but in every situation, by prayer and petition, with thanksgiving, present your requests to God."

[7] Hebrews 11:6 (NIV) "And without faith it is impossible to please God, because anyone who come to him must believe that he exists and that he rewards those who earnestly seek him".

[8] Psalm 37:4 (NIV) Take delight in the LORD, and he will give you the desires of your heart".

[9] Genesis 1:28 (NIV) "God blessed them and said to them, "Be fruitful and increase in number; fill the earth and subdue it. Rule over the fish in the sea and the birds in the sky and over every living creature that moves on the ground."

[10] Philippians 4:8 "Finally, brothers and sisters, whatever is true, whatever is noble, whatever is right, whatever is pure, whatever is lovely, whatever is admirable—if anything is excellent or praiseworthy—think about such things."

[11] 1 Corinthians 15:58 "Therefore, my dear brothers and sisters, stand firm. Let nothing move you. Always give yourselves fully to the work of the Lord, because you know that your labor in the Lord is not in vain."

[12] John 6:35 "Then Jesus declared, "I am the bread of life. Whoever comes to me will never go hungry, and whoever believes in me will never be thirsty.""

---

[13] John 7:38 "Whoever believes in me, as Scripture has said, rivers of living water will flow from within them."

[14] John 15:5 "I am the vine; you are the branches. If you remain in me and I in you, you will bear much fruit; apart from me you can do nothing."

[15] See Genesis 4

[16] See Judges 4

[17] See John 4

[18] Psalms 1:3 "On each side of the river stood the tree of life, bearing twelve crops of fruit, yielding its fruit every month. And the leaves of the tree are for the healing of the nations."

[19] Romans 14:13 "Therefore let us stop passing judgment on one another. Instead, make up your mind not to put any stumbling block or obstacle in the way of a brother or sister."

[20] Genesis 19:26 "But Lot's wife looked back, and she became a pillar of salt."

[21] Romans 12:3 "For I say, through the grace given unto me, to every man that is among you, not to think of himself more highly than he ought to think; but to think soberly, according as God hath dealt to every man the measure of faith.

[22] Psalm 23:3(emphasis added) "he refreshes my soul. He guides me along the right paths for his name's sake."